A Rookie reader®

Moving Day

Written by Jo S. Kittinger

Illustrated by Ilene Richard

SCHOLASTIC INC.

New York Toronto London Auckland Sydney
Mexico City New Delhi Hong Kong Buenos Aires

For Joan Broerman, who started me writing and kept me writing
—J.S.K.

To my wonderful family
—I.R.

Reading Consultants

Linda Cornwell
Literacy Specialist

Katharine A. Kane
Education Consultant
(Retired, San Diego County Office of Education
and San Diego State University)

ISBN 0-516-24472-8

12 11 10 9 8 7 6 5   3 4 5 6 7 8/0

Printed in the U.S.A.   61

First Scholastic paperback printing, September 2003

Pack my clothes.

3

Pack my toys.

5

Say good-bye to the girls and boys.

Load the truck.
Load the car.

Our new home is very far.

11

Stop for gas.
Stop for dinner.

Play a game.
I'm the winner!

15

Here's our town.

Here's our street.
Are there any kids to meet?

Here's our house.
There's so much space.

I think I'm going to like this place!

Word List (50 words)

a	for	I'm	our	there
and	game	is	pack	there's
any	gas	kids	place	think
are	girls	like	play	this
boys	going	load	say	to
car	good-bye	meet	so	town
clothes	here's	moving	space	toys
day	home	much	stop	truck
dinner	house	my	street	very
far	I	new	the	winner

About the Author

Jo S. Kittinger, a native of Florida, lived in several states before settling in Alabama. A love of books and a passion to create inspires Jo to write both fiction and nonfiction books for children. Jo enjoys pottery, photography, and reading in her spare time. While teaching her own children to read, Jo realized the critical role of emergent readers. She wrote this book while moving her son, Robert, into college.

About the Illustrator

Ilene Richard was a successful jewelry designer before getting back to illustrating children's books. She has illustrated many books in both the trade and educational markets. Ilene lives with her husband Lawrence, her daughter Jodi, her son Corey, and their dog Bess in Andover, Massachusetts.